A GUIDE TO LOVING

Also by Jack Dominian:

ONE LIKE US
LET'S MAKE LOVE
LIVING LOVE

A GUIDE TO LOVING

FOR YOUNG AND OLD

Jack Dominian

DARTON · LONGMAN + TODD

First published in 2005 by
Darton, Longman and Todd Ltd
1 Spencer Court
140–142 Wandsworth High Street
London SW18 4JJ

ISBN 0 232 52609 5

A catalogue record for this book is available from
the British Library.

Designed and produced by Sandie Boccacci
Phototypeset in 12/18pt Joanna
Printed and bound in Great Britain by
CPI Bath

CONTENTS

INTRODUCTION:
THE KEY TO HAPPINESS

THE 1960s USHERED IN a dramatic revolution in marriage and sexuality which destabilised moral standards that had prevailed for centuries. Society as a whole has not really known how to handle or respond to the increase in sex outside marriage and the widespread marital breakdown of recent decades, and the consequences have been devastating.

When I was working as a psychiatrist in the 1970s in the London borough of Brent – an area of great social deprivation – I found that the high incidence of depression I encountered was often linked to relationship problems, with children in turn suffering the detrimental effects of parental conflict. I realised that relationship discord and breakdown were at the heart of the distress I encountered daily in families.

In the absence of a new morality, in talking about

relationships parents, teachers and religious leaders have often been reduced to reiterating traditional prohibitions on sex outside marriage. These prohibitions are largely ignored by people both inside and outside the churches, especially young people, and have led to an increasing disenchantment with Christianity.

Should we abandon the Christian tradition when it comes to talking about sex, love and marriage? No – quite the opposite. My experience as a psychiatrist has shown me that at the core of Christian teaching is a message that is the key to good relationships and to happiness and fulfilment for all, whether believer or unbeliever, Christian or Muslim, young or old.

Christian teaching is not essentially about prohibitions and negatives. At its heart is a positive – *love*. The central belief of Christianity is that God is love. Christians believe that out of the abundance of this love God created the world and each one of us. God wants us to love him in this life and to be happy with him in the next. How do we love God? Through prayer and worship. And through loving our neighbour – in particular, of course, our partner and our children.

Christians believe that when we love our partner, our parents or our children we are in the presence of God. Every moment of authentic human loving is an act of prayer, for God is love.

> My dear friends,
> let us love one another,
> since love is from God
> and everyone who loves
> > is a child of God and knows God.
> Whoever fails to love does not know God,
> because God is love.
> > (1 John 4:7–8)

Love is at the heart of everyone's life, whatever our religious beliefs, whatever our age. It is a huge subject, but in this small book I will attempt to outline its essentials in a way that will meet the needs of these changing times.

Jack Dominian

FRC Psy, FRCP ED, D Sc (Hons), MBE

CHAPTER ONE

THE FOUNDATIONS

Childhood

There is no definition of love that can remotely do justice to its richness. The nearest way we can attempt to understand it is by describing the experiences we have as children. It is in our childhood that we receive the first experience of love. However, most of us do not remember our childhood very well, and even when we do, we are not equipped to analyse our experience and what it taught us. So love remains a mystery. But more than a hundred years of psychology have taught us a great deal about the early years of life, and we are indebted to Freud and many others since for putting the puzzle together.

Attachments

Immediately after birth we begin our love life by forming an attachment to our mother. Attachments are essential links which bind us first to our mother, then to our father, brothers or sisters if we have any, and to other significant people in later life.

Usually our mother is the first person with whom we form this bond. We do this through vision, sound and touch. We begin to recognise her face and then other parts of her body. We become familiar with her voice, and most important of all, we touch her and she holds us. These physical connections are laden with feelings: they are affective bonds. Within a few weeks we are bonded to her – we are dependent for our survival on her presence. This survival is about more than being fed – it is an emotional nourishment that makes us feel safe and content. Everyone knows what happens when as young children we lose sight of our mother. We become restless and start to cry. Crying is the human signal of distress, and the means of recalling our mother or any other person with whom we have an affective attachment.

Later on in life, whenever we fall in love or make a deep friendship, we form a new affective attachment. We are attracted by the appearance and sound of another, and want to be in their physical presence and hold them. This attachment is basic to loving. When we lose the people we love we are sad – we cry and mourn their departure, just as as a child we cried in the absence of key figures in our lives.

Within the attachment we feel safe and secure. We experience pleasure and gratification. The pleasure is linked early on with breastfeeding and with being held and gazed at. If we observe the interaction between a mother or father and their child, there is a reciprocal rhythm of bodily contact, smiling, and talking. Before children talk, they make appropriate sounds which are incomprehensible in terms of language, but meaningful as a loving response. At the heart of this love is intimacy which is both physical and emotional. Later, we shall see that falling in love and loving is a return to this physical and emotional intimacy. All friendships and marriage are expressions of this closeness. The difference between friendship and marriage is that in the latter there is a genital sexual dimension. Before Freud, nobody linked sexuality with childhood, but in the closeness between child and parents there is a physical gratification which psychologists describe as sexual. This tells us that sex and love are linked from the beginning of our lives.

Trust

Within the attachment just described, the child learns the rudiments of trust. Trust is experienced physically and emotionally. Physical trust is conveyed through feeling safe in the presence of our mother or father when being held by them. The opposite is felt where there is physical or sexual abuse, which causes physical and emotional damage. Children are totally dependent on their parents for their safety, hence the revulsion we feel when children are molested.

Later on, when we learn to talk, trust has to be established through the exchange of truth between adults and children. As we learn to trust our parents, we expect they will safeguard us emotionally by giving us the appropriate affection, and intellectually by telling us the truth.

As adults, love requires that we trust the person we love to respect our bodies, minds and feelings. Trust plays an important role in loving in all human relationships. We feel betrayed by anyone who lets us down, but particularly by those who love us, because we expect from them the same reliable care that we received from our parents.

Autonomy

Little by little, as young children, we begin to separate from our mother and father. Initially we will crawl a few yards away and then return to the safety of our mother's presence. Gradually we begin to let her out of sight for longer periods, returning to her only when we are frightened, hurt, or a stranger arrives.

Slowly we learn to walk, dress, feed ourselves and talk. In all these respects we are acquiring autonomy. This is the first stage in life when the balance between closeness and separation is learned. We will cope by ourselves for increasingly longer periods, playing on our own or with other children, away from the key parental figure. We will then return to base: to mother, father, granny, or to whoever is our principal attachment figure. In psychological terms we will increasingly learn to internalise our mother: to keep her presence alive inside ourselves despite her physical absence.

The same thing applies to adult friendship or love. We spend a lot of our time with the person we love, but we also have to spend time apart. The degrees of distress we experience in the absence of those we love depends on how much they matter to us, and how well we have internalised them. When we feel they are safe inside us, we can be separate from them for long periods without worry. Some people find it difficult to let the people they love out of their sight. When the beloved is out of sight they become anxious or frightened. These people do whatever they can to keep their partner near them. They are called possessive or jealous. Jealousy is the fear of losing someone we love, and it goes back to our childhood fear of losing our key attachment figure, which is usually our mother.

But most people find a balance between closeness and separateness, and this reflects the presence and absence of parental figures in the early years of life.

Conflict

When we are frustrated we get angry. Anger and love are closely linked, and are the opposite sides of the same coin. Some psychologists locate the roots of frustration and anger in the first few months of life. But it is usually in the second and third year, the years of the beginning of autonomy, that anger is seen most clearly. We want to do things our own way, our mother says 'no', and there is conflict. If we persist, our parents may shout or even smack, and there is a temporary rupture of the relationship. After a few seconds or minutes there is reconciliation, forgiveness and reparation.

As adults we say and do things that hurt those we love. At that moment, just like the child, we experience hurt: we lose contact with the person we love and we feel guilty. After a little while we forgive or are forgiven, we make amends and the relationship is restored.

School

At about the age of five, we go to school, having mastered the ability to separate from our mother. We have a certain independence: language command, the ability to take initiatives and the ability to play on our own. Up to a point we are self-reliant. We are ready to acquire the three R's. Now cognitive training begins in earnest.

Up until then our self-esteem – our ability to feel appreciated, loved, wanted and recognised – has grown with our parents' nurturing. During the school years, self-esteem will also be built on the results of industry and achievement. School, with its marks, reports and examination results, offers a visible indication of success or failure.

Self-esteem can now be built both on feeling loved by parents and teachers, and on the results of school work. This dual basis of self-esteem, coming from both home and school, has important implications for adult love. If we do not acquire the feeling of unconditional love on the basis of being a person worthy of love in our own right, then love and approval become solely dependent on achievement. The consequence of this is that in adult relationships we do not expect to be loved for our own worth. Every bit of approval has to be earned through performance. Husbands or wives who have been brought up in this way expect to be appreciated only when they fulfil their roles at home and at work. Their understanding of love is based on achievement, and they can only enjoy approval when they feel they have earned it. Such men and women can become workaholics, or become obsessed with keeping extremely neat and tidy households. Their whole life of love is based on a contract. They expect to discharge their responsibilities to the full, and be praised or criticised according to results. They can be extremely critical of themselves and of their partner if either of them fail to deliver the appropriate and required behaviour.

'It's Not Fair'

Between the ages of seven and ten, we reach a point of development when we no longer accept the authority of our parents unconditionally. We begin to argue back and to question our parents' absolute authority. We expect justifying reasons for rules and regulations, and feel unfairly treated when our parents use their authority without adequate reason. These are the years when homes and classrooms reverberate with the protest, 'It's not fair.'

The feeling of being asked to do something that does not respect our integrity, or is exploitative in any way, forms a deep groove in our emerging personality. Our whole sense of justice is linked with it. We expect to have our rights respected, to be treated fairly and to have our integrity safeguarded by everyone, and especially by those who claim to love us. This is why we feel particularly hurt when we are let down by those close to us. In letting us down, they can elicit our deepest anger.

Puberty and Adolescence

The beginning of the second decade is the time when puberty commences. This is the time when the secondary sexual characteristics appear and sexuality focuses on genitalia. Simultaneously the incest taboo appears and normally the emerging young boy or girl will not countenance sexual relations with parental figures. Freud claimed as a universal finding that a little boy is attracted sexually to his mother in his early years. The famous Oedipal complex is resolved at about the age of five when these wishes are abandoned and the child moves towards his father, on whose maleness he bases his development. The same thing is said to happen with the girl in the opposite direction. Be that as it may, puberty is the time of overt prohibition of incestuous relationships. Sadly these boundaries are sometimes broken by parents or relatives, and sexual abuse can occur at puberty or even before.

With the arrival of puberty there also comes adolescence, which is a time when young people slowly begin to separate from their parents. They find independent work, or continue with higher studies, and begin to be interested sexually, usually in someone of the opposite sex and for a few in someone of the same sex.

This is the time when courtship starts, and we begin a series of emotional and sexual encounters until we find someone with whom we fall in love. Sometimes we fall in love with more than one person, until one emerges as the chosen one, and marriage or cohabitation begins.

Marriage

Traditionally marriage has been seen as the institution where adults have sex from which children are conceived, and the whole cycle of life begins afresh. Today sex and children are still at the centre of matrimony, but much more is expected of it. Increasingly, men and women come together and want to experience love through each other. Marriage becomes the second intimate love relationship in life. But instead of finding love, a number of marriages break up and end in divorce.

There are many reasons for divorce. Some of them are to be found in the fact that in the course of our first intimate relationship of love, many of us have been hurt or wounded. We carry these emotional wounds into marriage and there, in the intimacy of this second loving relationship, we relive the difficulties, frustrations and anger of our childhood experiences. Since we usually have forgotten the hurts of our childhood, we are surprised to find that we are not getting along with our husband or wife. We find instead that we are quarrelling, feeling frustrated and alienated, our sex life is suffering, and ultimately we want to go. The reason for this is often because we are experiencing our partner as the disappointing, hurting, rejecting parental figure of the past. We do not know this because the past is unconscious, but sometimes we link past and present. One of the greatest contemporary challenges to marriage is to recognise and link the hurts of the past with the current difficulties of loving.

Hurt Childhood

A normal childhood should give us the feeling that we are loveable and good. That is to say, we should emerge in adult life with sufficient self-esteem to feel recognised, wanted and appreciated simply because we exist. Everyone who has received unconditional love feels some of these things. At the other end of the spectrum, we may feel unlovable, have low self-esteem and be very hungry for affection. In general, there are small minorities at either end of the spectrum with most people somewhere in the middle.

When we veer towards the negative side, we

have difficulty in persuading ourselves that anyone wants or appreciates us. We are constantly surprised when people find us attractive and want our company. We feel shy and lack confidence, and are extremely grateful for the slightest notice given to us. We expect criticism, but when we receive it, we are doubly hurt because we have no reserves of good feeling to cushion it. We may get excessively angry over trivial upsets, and shout and scream. On the other hand, we may bury our anger and become depressed.

As hurt people, we are excited when we are befriended, but expect to be abandoned very easily. When we receive love, we feel that at long last our needs are being met, only to discover that we find it difficult to accept. We end up pushing away those who love us.

When these points are explained to men and women who have difficulties in their relationships, they are astonished. Some of them realise their childhood was not ideal, but they still felt 'loved' by their parents. Others think it is their own fault: their parents gave them everything and it is they who made a mess of things.

In practice, of course, it is not always the

parents' fault. In any case, fault is the wrong word. As parents they offered their children the best that was available at the time. But parents are not the only contributors to love. Genes play a part. Our capacity to receive love depends on our make-up, and some people can receive affection much more easily than others. So the love we feel as adults is a mixture of the parenting we receive and our genes.

Nevertheless, many are still surprised when they are faced with the possibility that their parents were not as loving as they thought they were. When they begin to examine the matter in detail they may find that, while their parents took care of them physically and educationally, feeding and clothing them, providing them with adequate material benefits and sending them to good schools, nevertheless, they did not feel close to one or both parents.

The parents may have found it difficult to demonstrate affection, and the children were rarely picked up, hugged or caressed. Feelings may have rarely been displayed. Both parents may have worked and had little time for the children, or the children may have been sent to boarding schools from an early age. The parents may never have been satisfied with their children's performance, and criticism may have been rampant and approval or appreciation scarce. The children may have felt ignored for long periods, and were only noticed when they broke some rule.

Most people can recognise overt physical brutality. Many more wounds are inflicted by the absence of affection and affirmation in subtle ways, such as when parents prefer one brother or sister to another. Whatever the reason, there are many people who emerge from their childhood without the experience of unconditional love, and this becomes a handicap when they are expecting to be loved, or when they try to love others.

More specifically we can identify some particular patterns of hurt from individual phases of development.

Disorders of Attachment

As we have already seen, the capacity to form a bond is fundamental to loving. There are people who find it difficult to form an attachment. Having formed one, they live with the constant fear of losing their loved one, or being abandoned by them. They form what are known as 'anxious attachments' rooted in jealousy and possessiveness. Such men and women live with the constant dread of being left, and every other person is a threat to their relationship. They imagine their partner is having affairs when they are doing nothing of the sort, and they are overwhelmed with panic and desperation when they are. They expect to be supplanted with extraordinary ease, and all that the husband or wife has to do is to look at another woman or man and there is hell to pay. Often these people are not only anxious about being abandoned, but also live with the dread that something terrible will happen to their loved ones. If their partner is a little late in coming home they are overwhelmed with premonitions of tragedy.

Given this anxiety, they long to be physically close to their partner, and when this is not possible, to be in telephone or e-mail contact. Their hunger for physical closeness makes them possessive, and they dread letting their partner out of their sight. Their partner feels a prisoner and finds it difficult to do things alone.

The need for the physical presence of another person is a normal requirement of companionship, and is part of loving, but this hunger for the presence of the partner is an expression of excessive anxiety. Very often such a person is satisfied with the mere physical presence of their partner in the house. They rarely want to do anything with them provided they are physically available. They are often criticised by their partner who stays in the home, only to find them asleep or busy with some activity, and not remotely interested in them.

Disorders of Trust

Trust is fundamental for all human relationships, but particularly for those who are in an intimate loving exchange. In fact, trust is essential for our survival. It is relevant to physical closeness. We need to feel that we are not going to be hurt by those to whom we entrust our body. Therefore, all physical and emotional violence is a violation of love. Since loving intimacy expects sexual intercourse, trust is essential at the moment we abandon all our defences and become physically united.

Emotionally, trust is the foundation of the continuity of our loving relationship with another human being. If physical trust is the basis of our safety, then emotional trust is essential for the hope that we will continue to be loved.

Our capacity for emotional trust may be strong

or weak. A person whose ability to trust is weak may be suspicious, cynical, and expect very little out of life. They may emerge from a childhood in which they have had little reason to feel that anyone was reliable or trustworthy. Their parents promised, but did not fulfil: were inconsistent; said one thing and did another and told lies. They grew up expecting to be let down, and every person is a potential source of further hurt. This hurt is experienced particularly from those who are close to them when they fail to recognise them, appreciate them or make them feel wanted. The range of feeling after being let down is infinite, but it is especially pronounced when the partner has an affair. It may be very difficult to regain trust after an affair, and it may never return to its previous levels.

Trust is also essential in communication. If normal life is to continue, we must believe those who relate to us, and particularly those who claim to love us. If they tell us lies, half-truths or hide essentials from us, they lay foundations for distrust, which is corrosive to a loving relationship. Very often we tell lies because we are afraid that we will hurt the person we love, or that they will be angry with us. When a lie follows a lie, the situation becomes unsustainable, and the final position is much worse than if we had told the truth and faced the consequences.

Disorders of Autonomy

Autonomy is linked with our freedom and independence. When we commit ourselves to loving one person, we are at the same time reducing our freedom to form an exclusive relationship with someone else. We accept the responsibility of faithfulness. Furthermore, central to loving is offering our availability. We offer our body, mind and feelings to the one to whom we make our exclusive commitment. These restrictions are self-imposed and are usually accepted as the necessary conditions for the unique loving intimacy of marriage.

But we may have problems in this area. We may have had parents who were domineering, possessive, exacting, demanding and over-bearing. Our freedom and independence may have become particularly precious in our life. We may want the advantages of intimacy, but resent the restrictions on our freedom and independence. So, particularly in the early years of marriage, we enjoy sex, caring and affection, but want to go on as if we were single and use time to suit our own purposes. We go home for food and sex, and use the rest of the time to work, play and amuse ourselves with our friends. We have no time to meet the needs of our partner. When he or she is critical, we become angry and describe the requests as demands. Such people treat their partner as a restricting and demanding parent, against whom they angrily rebel.

Every satisfactory loving relationship has to work out a balance between availability and autonomy, dependence and independence, closeness and separation. On the one hand, couples can be so close and dependent on each other that they are described as 'fused'. These couples cannot do anything independently, and rely entirely on each other. Each lives by the kind permission of the other, feeling that they are incomplete without the other. Alternatively, some couples can be so independent that they hardly come near each other. Extremely independent relationships are the basis for so-called 'open' marriages, in which the partners agree to have the freedom to have a series of extramarital relationships without the other partner minding.

Disorders of Industry

The point has been already made that self-esteem is built on the unconditional love given by parents, and on work achievement. When children lack the feeling of being loved on the basis of their intrinsic worth, they fall back on the conditional love which they earn through their industry, and their adult relationships become contracts of mutual benefit. Instead of feeling wanted for their own sake, partners may do things for each other on a contractual basis, saying to each other 'I'll do this for you, if you'll do that for me.'

If for some reason these men or women are not in a position to be productive (for example, if they become unemployed), they lose their self-esteem completely. An alternative distortion is the person who works excessively as the sole basis for finding their value, and takes no pleasure in spending time with their partner or children.

Disorders of Dependence

The whole of childhood is a gradual separation from parental figures and those in authority. It is a movement of gradual independence, in which young people learn to decide, cope, handle fear, plan, anticipate, and overcome threats to their survival. They emerge as autonomous, self-reliant, self-governing and self-directing.

Some people achieve physical and intellectual maturity without an equivalent emotional one. They look and behave like adults, but feel unsure, uncertain, frightened, and still feel they need to rely on somebody stronger than themselves.

Marriages between such an emotionally dependent person and one who appears strong, dominant and assertive are common. The dependent person can be of either sex, and marries for security in the widest sense of the word.

With the passage of time, such dependent people grow up and realise their emotional potential. They no longer need their partner to make decisions for them on where to go and what to do; to help them to make up their minds; to shape their opinion and set their values. They no longer idealise or magnify the importance of their partner, and can make an equal contribution to the relationship. This is the best outcome of this kind of relationship, but there are alternative and dangerous ones.

The most common problem with such a relationship is that the dependent partner will outgrow their 'parental' partner. When they have attained their confidence, they will no longer need the security of their partner. These men and women may come to claim that they are no longer in love with their partner and that their 'love' was linked with their dependence. When that disappears, so does their love, and the marriage comes to an end.

Another problem is that the so-called 'strong' person behaves in an assertive, driving and domineering way, but that behind this 'strength' there may be an equally needy and emotionally deprived person. There comes a time when the dominant partner expresses underlying needs and yearnings for support, affection and understanding. These moments may come when they are sick, under pressure, when things go wrong for them or when they lose a parent or a friend. They make signals for help, but their partner either fails to recognise these, or is incapable of helping. The dominant person is acceptable so long as they have no needs. If they do show their needy side, their dependent partner, who usually finds they have nothing to offer, is overwhelmed and may run away.

Viable Love

I have described and stressed the importance of distorted childhoods because the capacity to be a loving partner is now the key to a viable marriage.

In the past, a marriage was based on the fulfilment of roles. The husband was considered to be the wage earner, the head of the family and the family ambassador in the outside world. The wife was expected to be the child bearer, the child rearer and the person who looked after the house. Good marriages depended on the fulfilment of these roles and on staying faithful to each other. Love was not considered an essential ingredient for such an institution, though some or all of its characteristics might enter a particular relationship.

Nowadays marriages are entered into on the basis of a life-long relationship of love. The viability of marriages depends on the ability of each partner to replicate the other's experiences of childhood love, now expressed in an adult form. Most marital breakdown is the result of one or both partners failing to meet these expectations of love.

CHAPTER TWO

FALLING IN LOVE

DURING ADOLESCENCE a number of social and psychological situations occur which prepare young people to fall in love. They are in a state of separation from their parents and experience aloneness. This aloneness sensitises them to the need for togetherness. Beyond togetherness, men and women long for an independent home of their own in which they can organise and control their lives. Cohabitation or marriage, particularly the latter, is a sign of adulthood. Through marriage they can assume adult roles. Society is governed by married adults, a state to which most people aspire.

There is a preliminary form of courtship in which a variety of men and women are tried out. Ultimately someone is preferred and becomes special. At this stage, two people fall in love with each other.

Millions of words have been written to describe the state of being in love.

At the heart of falling in love is physical attraction. Both sexes are highly attracted by each other's bodies. Although there is some agreement about physical beauty, the special attraction of another's physical appearance cannot be defined. Attraction is based on a whole variety of factors. But it should be noted that vision (finding the other pleasing to the eyes), sound (being attracted by their voice) and touch (enjoying being held by them) are all essential.

Physical excitement is stimulated by the same elements as those that form the attachment between ourselves and our mother. Falling in love is a resuscitation of the physical and emotional links which form our primary emotional attachment to our mother. It is a repeat in adult life of our infantile bonds.

Emotionally, we need to have the sense of feeling special to each other, recognised, wanted, needed and appreciated. The person we fall in love with makes us feel that we matter to them.

Beyond physical and emotional attraction, there is social fitness. We are usually attracted by people who are of the same intelligence and have the same interests, values and opinions. So to summarise, we are usually attracted by someone we like physically, emotionally and socially.

Once we have fallen in love, we are in a state of emotional excitement – a kind of ecstasy. We tend to idealise the person we love. In other words, we tend to think of our beloved as the most attractive, desirable and suitable person in the world. We are not in a mood to find fault with them. If we detect shortcomings, we reduce their importance. If the beloved upsets us, we tend to forgive and forget quickly. We want to believe that there is nothing wrong with the one we love.

The state of idealised excitement elicits a marked desire for closeness and contact. We spend every possible minute with each other, and use the time when we are apart telephoning, texting and writing e-mails to each other. There is an enormous longing for unity and especially for sexual intercourse.

This state of falling in love is a prelude to marriage, or nowadays to cohabitation. The desire for the wonderful feeling of being in love to continue for the rest of one's life, and to be linked with the beloved, is the most natural thing in the world.

Despite this expectation, the sad reality is that many marriages do not last and end in divorce. So are there any clues during the period of courtship as to whether the person we love will stay with us forever?

There is no certain way of making sure that the person we fall in love with is likely to turn out to be a stable, reliant and trustworthy lover for the next fifty years – but there are some clues. In particular, we should consider their ability to be loving people. We should pay special attention to their backgrounds, not only for their social suitability, but also for their emotional stability. Broken homes and evidence of parents with drinking problems should ring warning bells. However, we have seen that however stable the parents, their offspring can still grow up feeling unloved.

So it is the quality of the personality that should forewarn us. Are they reliable, trustworthy, consistent? Do they tell the truth? Even more important, are they particularly sensitive to criticism, unsure of themselves and lacking confidence? Do they get easily hurt, react frequently and seriously to any rejection, lose their temper often and seem to want to be in control? Must they have their way? Are they uncompromising, frequently critical and hurtful and rarely appreciative?

After a quarrel do they find it difficult to make up? Are they jealous or possessive? Everyone has some of these traits, but it is important to note the frequency and intensity of these characteristics. If they appear frequently and are marked, then they are clearly warning signals that they will remain present in the relationship after marriage.

At the social level, stability is shown by an average or good school and work record. In particular, one should watch out for frequent changes of work, long periods of unemployment, failure to persist with a given task, the way they respond to stress of any sort and any evidence of marked drinking, gambling and drug taking.

If everyone with these characteristics was rejected for marriage, there would be many people who would never marry. If the person with whom we have fallen in love has some of these traits, we should warn ourselves in advance. Our love will certainly overcome many difficulties, but we have to ask ourselves about our ability to cope with disappointments, frustrations and periods of feeling rejected and unloved. Above all, if we decide to take on a markedly hurt person as our partner for life, we should realise that there will certainly be problems in our relationship. If we feel vulnerable, unsure of ourselves and fragile in our capacity to feel loveable, then we need to choose someone who is not equally vulnerable. Otherwise we will find that, after the excitement of being in love, both of us will be hungry for love, and neither will have the required resources to meet each other's needs. If we are vulnerable and hungry for love, it is better for us to choose someone whose own background makes them more capable of meeting our needs.

When people are in love, they strive very hard to be on their best behaviour, and it is important to look at their background and their previous lifestyle to make a proper assessment of their personality. This is not at all easy, but it is necessary so that whatever choice is made, there should be some appreciation of the person who is going to emerge after the excitement and idealisation of being in love have dimmed.

CHAPTER THREE

LOVING

THERE IS PLENTY OF evidence, from both personal experience and research findings, that the excitement of falling in love subsides after a few years of marriage. Our idealisation of our beloved is replaced by a recognition of the reality of the person we are married to. When they are no longer on their best behaviour, their shortcomings will become apparent. Everybody has faults and limitations. Hopefully the good qualities outnumber the bad, but in the end, relationships will survive if both partners feel loved over the next fifty years: that is to say, recognised, wanted and appreciated.

Everybody knows and recognises the state of falling in love. The media, particularly television, bombard us with images of falling in love. Chocolates, coffee, sweets, clothes, toiletries, cars and a variety of services, are all sold on the basis of a boy falling in love with a girl. The buzz, excitement and thrill of boy meeting girl and feeling overwhelmed by her body and appearance (little is shown of the emotional and social exchange) is the bread and butter of public persuasion. Novels, films and TV soaps are built on the vagaries of falling in and out of love.

But little is shown or written about the next stage of loving – year in, year out, over four, five or six decades. In many ways this is not surprising. It is during the twentieth century that medical advances and social changes have added some twenty years to the average life expectancy, with marriages enduring into the couples' seventies and eighties. Historically, couples have come together, reproduced, and when the offspring repeated the cycle, died. Today couples live for two or more decades after their children have grown up. From the time the excitement of 'falling in love' begins to wane until one of the couple dies, the relationship will be sustained on the basis of loving.

The four ingredients of loving are *sustaining*, *healing*, *growth* and *sexual intercourse*.

Sustaining
Being Available

At the centre of a loving relationship is the physical and emotional availability of the partners to each other. This availability involves being together and doing things together and, of course, with the children. Excessive work, long absences and a busy social life can all act as corrosives to love if we do not leave any time for each other. Remaining available for each other requires the willingness to make sacrifices of time, and of oneself.

Next to physical availability is practical availability. Love not only requires that we spend time with each other, but that we are ready to do things to meet each other's needs. Central to this is the willingness to work and provide material security for the family. In the past this was the task of the husband: today both men and women work. But in order for one or both to work, couples need to help each other with the household tasks of shopping, cleaning and cooking. How these tasks are shared depends on the individual needs of the couple. And beyond the routine work, the couple need to express their love by spoiling each other.

Availability is specially needed at times of stress:

pregnancy, caring for young children or elderly relatives, bereavement or life-threatening illness. Availability here means physical presence and time allocated to listen, encourage and offer sympathy and hope. All this availability is normally taken for granted, and given without grudge or resentment in a reliable and trustworthy way, but at the other end of the scale we may hear husbands or wives saying that their partner is never there, especially when needed, and even if they are, they can't be trusted to do anything properly. To be available not only requires effort and sacrifice to be physically present whenever we are needed, but also the willingness and desire to be of use. All this demands a sensitive awareness of the needs of our partner and children. Children make their needs clear reasonably easily. Our partner is not always so easily read. They may appear to be endlessly ready to be available and do things for us, while they clearly need relief and support. Constant vigilance is needed to ensure that we are present and available when we are needed.

Communicating

Being available is the background of love, but the quality of the exchange between partners is the next step of loving.

At the centre of this next stage is communication. We communicate what we feel in a variety of ways: by being present or absent; by buying and doing things for those we love; by thinking about them and by keeping in touch. But above all, we sustain our love by words.

In speaking, we express our thoughts and convey our feelings of interest, concern, affection, worry, anger and inquiry. But communication is a dialogue. We not only have to speak, but we also need to listen, both to what is expressed rationally and to the 'feeling' content of the speaker. If we listen to words and do not hear the 'feeling' message then we are deaf. It is vital that we hear the scream of distress as well as the shout of jubilation. In listening, we have to give our partner the chance to express what they feel, and not prejudge it by saying at the beginning of a comment: 'Not again. We've been over that a thousand times.' If our partner is returning to a theme, their preoccupation with it means that we have not really 'heard' it. Another way of being deaf is simply waiting for the partner to stop speaking so that we can start, without hearing what they have said. Sometimes people find it difficult to say what they feel because they are afraid to hurt us. It is important to encourage our partner to tell us what they feel, even if it causes us pain, because this is the way to negotiate and overcome difficulties. We both have to have the courage and confidence to say what we feel so that we can face the truth.

Women are much better at communicating and using words than men. Men may find it difficult to express themselves in this way, and when pushed will say that when women talk they are 'nagging'. Men may keep silent and in this way never show their feelings for their partner, but communication is central to loving; and it is the way we keep each other in touch with our inner world.

Showing Affection

Communicating with words is one way of showing love, but showing affection more widely is essential to loving. We can show affection by saying affectionate things to each other, touching, hugging, kissing, and helping each other at difficult times. Physical contact is often confined to sexual exchanges, but it should be remembered that physical affection is a demonstration of closeness, reassurance, mutual trust and active concern for each other. It is the means of reminding ourselves at regular intervals that we remain special to each other. At times this physical closeness will be expressed by an evening together, a weekend spent away from home, or a holiday. All these are helpful, but we can show affection by a spontaneous hug at any time.

Affirming

Beyond communication and affection, we need to be affirming people. At the extreme end of not being affirming are people who are silent when things go well and critical when things go wrong. Such people rarely praise, appreciate or encourage, but expect to motivate others through criticism, inducing guilt or making them feel bad.

Genuine loving occurs when we start by appreciating the good there is in our partner, and move on from that moment of affirmation to constructively criticise what is defective. In this way, we are always building on the resources our partner already has instead of casting doubt on their value. At the centre of much marital breakdown is the highly critical exchange between partners: 'Whatever I do is wrong. I can never please him or her.' This is the recurrent cry of those who find it difficult to remain in a relationship any longer. We should examine our consciences, not by asking ourselves what we have done wrong, but by asking ourselves when we last affirmed our partner and built up their self-esteem.

Affirmation can be given in a variety of ways: appreciating a new dress, praising a good meal, celebrating success achieved at work, examinations passed, difficulties negotiated or anything well done. In the nature of things, major achievements do not happen frequently, but we can affirm the effort and thought that goes into our partner's caring for us all the time.

A number of people find it difficult to show their appreciation in words, and do so by deeds and buying gifts. These are alternatives and have their place, but love cannot be bought. It needs to be a personal experience of being appreciated, and the right word at the right time means a great deal more than all the jewels in the world.

Healing

In previous sections I have shown that, due to a combination of genetic factors and upbringing, many people grow into their adult life as wounded people. In one sense we are all wounded people, but what matters is the intensity of our difficulties. At the extreme end of these problems are those who seek solutions in drink, drugs, gambling, promiscuity or crime. Since these people are a minority, we tend to label them as abnormal, and take refuge in considering ourselves normal. But the facts belie this comfortable belief. Research in the last two decades has shown that violence and sexual abuse in the family is common. We may say that we do not beat our wives and abuse our children, but hitting someone is so common that we do not consider ourselves unusual when we have done it.

Even when we know that we do none of these things, we need to search deeper and look at other common patterns of behaviour. Let us look at our self-esteem. How confident do we feel? How sure do we feel of our value? When we are praised, do we turn away in embarrassment because we do not believe that we are worth much? If we do not feel of value, it is scarcely surprising that we do not show appreciation of others. We cannot give what we have not got ourselves. We can only concentrate on our faults and those of others because our inner world is a mass of negativity.

Do we feel loveable? Or are we someone who

deep inside feels there is nothing loveable in them, and can only earn appreciation by perpetually doing things? Are we a man who has no sense of unconditional love, and can only find justification in being a provider? Are we a woman who also knows little about being unconditionally loveable, and relies on her role as a house-wife or mother to earn her husband's approval? Do we find our meaning from what we do or from the person we are?

If we have no sense that we are intrinsically loveable, then we find it difficult to believe that we are of value unless we are productive. Even when we have a partner who loves us and a fulfilling lifestyle, we still feel empty. Men and women without a sense of personal value find it difficult to feel appreciated. Instead they seek the external excitements of alcohol, drugs, gambling, sex, power or public approval. When the buzz these can bring disappears, they feel flat and seek another round of stimulation. They may appear outwardly normal, but these are restless, unhappy men and women who find only short bouts of contentment.

Some of us are married to markedly wounded people, others to those whose wounds are less marked. The latter may nevertheless lack confidence, feel uncertain, be indecisive and feel easily lost and over-whelmed by adversity. They may be highly sensitive to criticism, need a lot of reassurance, get easily depressed and often wonder about the meaning of life. As a result, they may be irritable, quick-tempered, self-centred, withdrawn, moody, unpredictable, undemonstrative or mean with money.

In the face of this behaviour, we begin to label people. We call them 'difficult' or we are judgemental and describe them as lazy, selfish, self-centred, egotisti-cal, or generally nasty. A lot of angry exchanges between partners consist of a dialogue in which one partner says 'You're selfish' and the other replies 'I'm not'. This conversation, or something like it, can go on indefinite-ly. The alternative to being judgemental and critical with a partner is to leave them. As expectations of mar-ital love increase, more and more marriages break down when there is an encounter between two wounded people.

Instead of criticising or abandoning our partner, we can do one of two things. We can accept them as they are and adapt ourselves to their behaviour. This is what usually happens, providing their conduct is not too damaging or destructive.

But an even better way of loving is to respond to the wounds of our partner by recognising them as hurts and not as wilful and deliberate attacks upon us. Then we can give the wounded partner a healing response by providing them with stability to counteract their instability, trustworthiness to counteract their mistrust, unconditional acceptance to counteract their sense of rejection and approval to counteract their sense of being criticised. In other words, we can give them a different experience to that which they had as children. Such healing is not easy. These men and women are hungry for affection, approval and reassurance, but they find it difficult to trust and believe that anyone wants them. When they do feel loved they cannot retain the positive experience for long, so it needs frequent repetition.

The intimacy of a close relationship re-opens the wounds of earlier difficulties, but also gives the opportunity of healing which is one of the most powerful expressions of love. We all have opportunities to heal our spouse provided we recognise their awkwardness as an expression of hurt and avoid labelling them in a moralistic or judgemental sense. We can give them the level of experience they need. The wounded person in need must be receptive and open to learning a new way of being. The trouble is that we can get accustomed to our hurt, and get greater gratification by indulging in our misery than in changing towards wholeness. There are no short cuts to wholeness, happiness, inner peace and the removal of anxiety, but the intimacy of marriage is probably the most common way of achieving these ideals.

Here lies the crossroads between Christianity and the solutions of the world. In the case of Christianity, love requires the qualities of continuity and persistence in order that healing be brought about. The secular response can be marital breakdown, lack of commitment, impatience and disposability. The awkward partner is abandoned in the pursuit of another who is more acceptable.

Genuine Christian love recognises the importance of commitment, faithfulness and sacrifice, which are essential to overcome human difficulties. Some partners may be too destructive or damaging to continue living with. But this conclusion should only be reached as a last resort.

Conflicts and Quarrels

There are those who think that a quarrel between lovers is undesirable, and a sign that they do not love each other enough. In fact, couples may be divided into three categories: those who never quarrel, those who never cease to do so, and the vast majority, who have the occasional fight in between long periods of tranquil life.

Freud postulated that we all have the basic instincts of sexuality and aggression, and that our personality is built on the vicissitudes of these twin instincts. His successors were more appreciative of the development of love which is the infrastructure of this whole booklet.

Nevertheless, aggression is a basic human ingredient which is part of all our personalities. It is a capacity that is essential to our survival. When we are threatened physically, emotionally or socially, we usually respond with a flight or fight pattern of behaviour. We either give in and retreat or we fight for our physical, emotional or social integrity.

The most common reason for fighting is in order to survive, which means protecting our bodies, feelings, values and opinions. Fighting is not essential for our protection; it only becomes so when someone threatens the things we hold essential, precious or sacred.

Just because two people are married, it does not mean they necessarily agree on everything. In fact, as partners become more and more equal, they are much more likely to differ and to hold on to their own values and opinions.

Differences of opinion can arise when partners are planning journeys, buying a new home, making any decision that affects them both, or establishing the truth of something that concerns them both. Conflict may arise over communication when a partner is challenged about what they are supposed to have said and called a liar. Broken promises can cause disagreements, and when partners feel criticised, put down, humiliated or feel rejected or unloved they may respond with anger.

In all these situations each partner wants to assert their vision of the truth, the reasonableness of their position, the wisdom of their action, or the justification for their hurt. In each case, they are defending something important and precious, whether it is bruised bodies, hurt feelings or social embarrassment when the damage was inflicted in public. So conflict follows, and this can escalate in terms of abuse and potential physical damage when alcohol or drugs are involved.

A quarrel is a common way in which two people express their hurt, put forward their point of view, discharge their angry feelings and protect their interests. In the process of a quarrel something good may emerge when the anger is heard, felt and registered. In this way we appreciate the pain we have caused, and can learn in a new way to respect something precious in our spouse and avoid repeating our damaging behaviour. So conflict can be a way of reaching a deeper appreciation both of ourselves and those we love.

This is creative conflict, but there can also be sterile quarrelling when we simply let off steam, do not bother to listen to each other and are preoccupied in scoring points. In this type of quarrel partners take turns to win a battle. If one succeeds in defeating the other, the defeated person waits for an opportunity to take revenge, and so conflict becomes a power game of mutual ascendancy. In these circumstances, partners are waiting to prove each other 'wrong' or 'bad', and the conflict is a recurrent occasion for pouring forth venom, bitterness and spite.

The situation can deteriorate further when the quarrel is no longer an occasion to express anger, but an opportunity to be destructive. Anger imperceptibly turns to hate when the person we are supposed to love becomes the enemy we want to destroy. Physical and emotional battering, and in extreme cases murder, may follow. This is the other side of the coin of love.

What is the aftermath of conflict? Most frequently the couple forgive and forget and make up quickly. They have sent a message to each other, and want to resume a harmonious relationship. But this is not always the case. Some people feel bad and guilty when they become angry. They become extremely uncomfortable and withdraw into themselves for long periods. This is what is called sulking, but is in fact a complex phenomenon in which angry people feel unwanted, rejected and destructive, and find it difficult to live with themselves. They feel unlovable and, while they yearn to be forgiven and made to feel good again, they spurn all efforts towards reconciliation. When their partner tries to make up, touch or hug them, the partner is pushed away and they run off. They may

remain withdrawn for long periods, find it very difficult to apologise and even more difficult to accept
responsibility for any hurt they have caused.
Superficially this is interpreted as pride and the need
always to be right. In fact, these men and women have
such poor self-esteem that they find it intolerable to
openly admit wrongdoing. They cannot accept the
responsibility of being in the wrong because they
already feel that they are bad, cannot afford to condemn
themselves, and cannot tolerate any further criticism.
Such men and women often rouse our hostility because
of their stubbornness and unwillingness to accept
responsibility, and to behave in a mature way. In fact, in
spite of their adulthood, they are still behaving as hurt
children who feel bad and unwanted, and need rescu-
ing from their plight. This does not mean that the other
partner always has to apologise and make overtures for
peace. Sometimes this may be necessary, but it is more
important to reach out and reassure the fragile partner
that they are not considered bad: that what they have
said or done may be unacceptable, but they themselves
certainly are not, and their lovability remains unaltered.

Frequent and escalating quarrels may be a sign
that there is a real deterioration in the relationship of a

couple. Counsellors are used to hearing that increased quarrelling is the reason for a couple seeking help. This means that the hurt or needs of one partner are not being heard or healed by the other, and the situation is becoming increasingly unacceptable. The alternative to escalating quarrelling is increased withdrawal, with each partner growing indifferent or facing deepening depression. Suppressed anger often prompts a change of mood and leads towards depression and irritability. If this suppressed anger is not recognised then depression may be tackled wrongly and the underlying cause overlooked.

Growth

Loving someone for fifty years or more is a challenge. The excitement of the first few years of the relationship has to be replaced and sustained by a deeper and wider loving. During these years we change, and love has to overcome this process of change. In the course of time we may come to appreciate the person we married far more, or we may come to perceive them as shallow, empty and superficial, although we do not usually have a sudden revelation of new riches or a sudden awareness of poverty. Most relationships survive because the familiarity of a partner is a source of pleasure and joy, and we would not wish to be with another person. Children and shared experiences help to form new bonds with each other, and triumph over adversity gives us a new mutuality. But in the course of time we do change, and we have to face conflicting feelings over these changes.

Physically, with the passage of time, we move away from the freshness of youth to gaining weight and acquiring grey hair and the wrinkles of middle and old age. If we are dependent on the sexual and physical excitement of our twenties, then we may become disenchanted with the limitations of age. This happens especially when the marital bond is based on physical and sexual attraction and not on loving the whole person. When beauty wanes, then our partner's hold on us may also slacken. Authentic love requires that we cope with these changes, as well as the stress of illness, without losing the meaning that our partner gives us.

Intellectually we reach the pinnacle of our intelligence in our adolescence. Our IQ does not increase thereafter, but while our basic intelligence remains the same we can convert it into wisdom. We can learn, with the help of our partner and through discernment, to distinguish between glitter and gold. Our values may deepen and our priorities change. Instead of being over-attached to the drives of food, sex, wealth, making money and acquiring power over others, we can recognise that peace, justice and the needs of the poor, deprived and disabled, should become our priorities. We can alter course at any time in our life. We can change jobs, use our spare time for these causes or dedicate our lives to following a new direction. If our partner moves in this direction of altruism, it is part of loving to give them support in their new venture.

Over the years we can move up or down the social scale. We can succeed, achieve and be promoted or become unemployed, sick or disabled, or turn to alcohol and drugs. It is part of loving to remain committed to our partner whatever the changes in their life. Love is not dependent on social success. We are committed to a person, not the incidentals of their appearance or status or success. The secular word for this type of commitment is loyalty, but it is all part and parcel of the basic affectionate attachment to which I have repeatedly referred.

Against this permanency, with its continuous

attachment in varying circumstances, there are patterns of change in which spouses fall 'out of love' with each other. Reference has already been made to unions in which a partner starts a relationship because they are dependent, insecure or feel unlovable. With the passage of time, they become self-reliant, confident and begin to feel of value. Since the relationship was based on meeting a personal need of deprivation rather than on an affectionate attachment to the partner, when the need is no longer present, the relationship ceases to have meaning and is abandoned. Another pattern of fragility is a relationship based on the gratification of desires for sex, money or power. When these needs are no longer met, the so-called 'love' disappears and the marriage breaks down.

So change can increase love by deepening our awareness of, commitment to and availability to our partner, or it can remove the need for the other person. It is important when contemplating marriage to try to evaluate how much we love our future husband or wife. We need to evaluate whether we are forming an affectionate attachment based on their physical, emotional and social characteristics or buying resources to meet our sexual, emotional or social needs. The more needy and apparently desperate we are to link up with a particular person, the greater we should suspect our motives. There is a difference between feeling that another person will give us stability, encouragement and reassurance, and feeling that we will disintegrate without their presence in our life. In particular, we should be on our guard against poor self-esteem which makes us feel that the first person who pays us any attention is the only one we can marry because no-one else will look at us. The more careful we are about our initial choice, the less likely we are to marry out of need, which can be a transient experience in our life and can contribute to marital breakdown.

Sexual Intercourse

The fourth pattern of loving is sexual intercourse. Sexual intercourse is the channel through which sustaining, healing and growth are transmitted and reinforced. On each occasion, sexual intercourse gives life to the couple and occasionally new life arises.

Body Language

The body is a means of communication. We shake hands to indicate greetings and friendships. When we embrace and hug we show friendship, love and affection. Similarly, when we make love we talk to each other with our bodies. What do we say? We say at least five things:

1. We affirm our partner as the most important person in our lives. We recognise, trust, appreciate and want each other. Here, sexual intercourse is an act that affirms our identity.

2. When a man makes love to his wife he helps her to become fully feminine and when a woman makes love to her husband she helps him to become fully masculine. So, sexual intercourse affirms our sexual identity.

3. In the course of our intimate relationships, we argue, quarrel and hurt each other. Usually we forgive and forget quickly. Sometimes the pain is deeper and longer. After days or even weeks we make love. So, sexual intercourse can be an act of reconciliation.

4. As human beings one of our most important needs is to feel recognised, wanted and appreciated. When our spouse gives us a signal that they want to make love to us it is a moment of basic hope for our existence.

5. Finally, sexual intercourse is one of the most power-

ful ways of saying 'Thank you. Thank you for being
with me yesterday, today and hopefully tomorrow.'

The Spiritual Dimension

Sexual intercourse is an intensely pleasurable experience which gives life to the couple. Occasionally new
life arises as a result, and it can be a language rich with
interpersonal meaning. It is also a distinctly spiritual
experience. Christians believe that God is love, and that
when we are making love, we are entering and joining
with the very heart of God. Thus sexual intercourse is a
sacred act. It is in fact the most important recurrent act
of prayer for the couple.

When we think of this sacred significance, we
understand that sex requires a protective layer of human
circumstances which we have traditionally found in the
exclusive, continuous, faithful and permanent relationship of marriage. Sexual intercourse outside this frame-
work has traditionally been forbidden primarily
because of the danger of starting a new life without two
parents to support and nurture it, but we now see that
sex in all other circumstances lacks the appropriate
conditions to promote its unique human and sexual
meaning.

Another spiritual dimension of sexual intercourse is that sexual intercourse is an act in which two
people, a man and a woman, become one, totally united
in and through love and yet completely separate. What
does this remind us of? Nothing less than the Trinity.
Sexual intercourse is a recurrent act which allows the
couple to unite with the very depths of the most
profound mystery of the Christian faith.

Sexual Intercourse and Morality

In the past, sexual intercourse was confined to marriage
because its primary purpose was seen as biological, to
procreate: and children needed two parents. Today most
sexual intercourse is non-procreative and young people
want to know how it can be wrong to have sex outside
marriage or within a committed relationship of love. The
answer is that sexual intercourse is an act that has far
more meaning than physical pleasure. As we have seen,
physical attraction and pleasure are the basis for con-
veying love to someone whom we love and are
committed to. When love is absent, a great deal of the
meaning of the act is lost and human integrity suffers.

CHAPTER FOUR

PARENTS AND CHILDREN

FOR AT LEAST three thousand years in all religious traditions, including the Judaeo-Christian tradition, sexual intercourse has been linked with conceiving children. Today only a few sexual acts are needed to produce the average family of two children, and the majority of sexual intercourse is non-procreative.

Children are precious – whatever the size of the family, they become the visible sign of their parent's love – and they give their parents a new meaning in life. They become not just men and women and husbands and wives, but fathers and mothers.

Parental love is a spontaneous response to the helplessness of the child, who needs protection and nurturing. This nurturing is a reciprocal exchange, first between the mother and child, then in turn involving the father and other key people. In the first few months, the reciprocity is physical. The baby sleeps and feeds, and the mother takes pleasure in the baby's movements and responses. This relationship gradually evolves into smiling, mutual gazing and touching. Slowly the baby begins to hold its head up, and then its body, and in due course it will crawl, babble and show pleasure in a number of ways. Eventually the baby will learn to walk and talk, giving more pleasure to parents, and then begins the journey towards autonomy, with its mixed blessings of independence and chaos. Throughout the baby's childhood the parents will experience a mixture of joy and worry.

Parents not only supply the material needs of their child as far as they are able (this is harder in some parts of the world than in others), but another of their chief responsibilities is to give the child a sense of unconditional loving. This is done by ensuring that the physical, emotional, social and cognitive needs of the growing child meet a sensitive and accurate response. It is in the quality of this response that the child's feelings of security, trust, confidence, self-acceptance and permanence will depend. No parent is perfect, but most parents care intensely about their children and want to do the best for them.

In order for the parents to be as available as they can for their children, they need each other's love and support. In this respect sexual intercourse serves the needs of the children indirectly by constantly recharging their parents' love for each other.

It goes without saying that in order to give the children the best security and love available, the parents need a stable and loving relationship. Marital breakdown, although sometimes unavoidable, is a markedly destabilising factor.

Parenting

As a result of our increasing psychological understanding, we now know that the basis for the adult personality is largely but not exclusively laid down in the first two decades of life, and that parenting, especially in the early years, is of paramount importance. We particularly need to educate for love, the heart and centre of Christianity, and to emphasise the link between love and sex, because if we neglect this, we are wasting our time trying to lay down prohibitions in adolescence. The responsibility of parents lies much deeper than simply attending to their child's academic education. It also covers human growth, and particularly the understanding of how to handle emotions and the development of individual responsibilities. Growth is not confined to school, but goes on in every area of the child's life as the child persistently asks questions. The child's 'why' may sometimes stretch the patience of the parents but it is absolutely necessary to respond truthfully.

When it comes to personal education, in the past parents have been preoccupied with sexual behaviour, moral duty and avoiding pre-marital sex, but our emotional life is primarily about love and love occurs in the first intimate relationship of life. The early years are vital for learning how to be loved and nurtured, and how to take the first tentative steps in offering love.

I have already stressed the five elements of love, namely *closeness and availability* (both physical and emotional); *communication* (especially the ability to give and receive both cognitive and emotional messages); *demonstration of affection* physically and verbally (summarised in 'Show me, tell me, touch me'); *affirmation* (the oxygen of the child's life is to hear 'Well done!'); and the *resolution of conflict*.

Traditionally in society parenting is associated with providing discipline. Christianity in particular has been preoccupied with the presence of the devil and sin in our lives and the desire to root these out. It makes a great difference whether we see children as being fundamentally evil and in need of conversion, or fundamentally good but vulnerable because of an initial alienation from God caused by original sin, which can be healed with love. Needless to say, these attitudes have played vital roles in correction and punishment. Physical punishment has a long and enduring history in all societies and particularly in Christianity. Apart from its brutality, physical punishment has been shown repeatedly by psychology to be a powerful provocation towards violence in later life. So how can we discipline rightly?

What we are aiming for is to teach our children to understand that anger, envy, jealousy, hatred and greed damage not only the other person but also ourselves. Older children can understand this when it is explained. Younger children, especially the under-fives, who can get into temper tantrums, need to be taken away from the scene of the eruption, held safely and strongly until their tears dry up, and gently talked to at the level of their understanding. This is an appropriate method of teaching self-control and an opportunity for moral principles to be strongly instilled. In a young child, the feeling of being cut off from the love of their parents and from the paradise of their presence is a profound punishment in itself, and it is absolutely necessary to speed up the process of reconciliation and forgiveness. The young child can be asked 'What do you say?' and soon learns that the appropriate response is 'Sorry!' In older children and adults the sequence of anger, verbal and physical hurt, guilt, apology, reconciliation and forgiveness establishes a pattern for dealing with quarrels and conflicts.

Conservatives who love rules, regulations and punishment say that this is all very well, but that children need to know right from wrong. Indeed they do, for no other reason than their own safety and preservation is at stake, but this is not primarily a question of obedience to rules, although this can be necessary for avoiding physical danger, but of understanding how to love ourselves and our neighbours.

Obedience is a favourite word of authoritarians and in particular of enthusiastic Christians, who use Jesus as their principal example. They like to quote the example of the obedience that Jesus showed to his father. To interpret the word 'obedience' in an authoritarian sense is to introduce the concept of fear. This could not have been the basis of the obedience of Jesus, for according to St John:

> In love there is no room for fear,
> but perfect love drives out fear,
> because fear implies punishment
> and no one who is afraid
>> has come to perfection in love.
>
> (1 John 4:18)

I believe the real interpretation of Jesus' obedience is commitment based on love.

CHAPTER FIVE

LOVE IN THE SEXUAL WILDERNESS

THE ADVENT OF widespread contraception in western society, together with the acceptance by Christianity that sexual intercourse has a great deal more meaning than simply as a method for producing children has led to a virtual breakdown of traditional sexual morality – hence the title of this chapter.

Sex nowadays can take place under virtually any circumstances, and the average age of having sexual intercourse for the first time in Europe and the United States is around sixteen. Many are having sex at a much earlier age. Neither society nor Christianity has yet to devise an acceptable moral basis to guide young people regarding the appropriate circumstances under which sexual intercourse can occur.

Christianity still clings to the rule that sex

outside marriage is wrong but, since puberty begins at around thirteen or fourteen and the average age of marriage is about thirty, it is not surprising that this Christian teaching is largely ignored. In fact, the continued insistence on this rule has become a powerful reason for the withdrawal of young people from church attendance.

While some still adhere to keeping sexual intercourse within marriage, it is universally recognised that they are a distinct minority. In fact, there is only one alternative way of formulating a moral basis for sexual intercourse and this is to link it with love.

The Link of Sex with Love

What is the basis for linking sex with love? Sex is more than merely an encounter with another body which gives pleasure. It is an encounter with another *person*.

Sex does give pleasure, but this has a personal meaning. Remaining at the human level, this meaning, as already described, communicates personal significance, acceptance, trust, recognition, a minimum of care, appreciation, expression of affection and personal involvement.

Some argue that sex does nothing of the sort; it

is simply an act that gives pleasure. If that was so, the overwhelming majority of men and women would simply masturbate and, although men use prostitutes, the absence of a personal, intimate encounter under these circumstances is well understood and appreciated. Although a lot of effort has gone into stripping sexual intercourse of human meaning and rendering it merely a vehicle of pleasure, everybody knows that at the very least it is more than that, and at the very best it is a personal communication of love. Society is bristling with songs, plays and books, which speak of 'love', of 'wanting each other', of 'finding the right one', of 'coming home' and so on.

At a Christian level, the Book of Genesis tells us that we are created in the image of God who, according to St John, is love. When God had finished creating the world he saw all that he had made and 'indeed it was very good'. We need search no further for the link between sex and love, but it is seen in the Song of Songs, in the tradition of the prophets who saw marriage as a symbol of the covenant of love between Yahweh and his people, and in Paul's declaration that spouses are to love each other as Christ loved the Church. Finally, in my own description of sexual intercourse, both the humanistic and spiritual elements lead us to the concept of love.

Understanding Love

It is easier to describe the link of love with sex than to have an accurate sense of when love really is present in a relationship. The following outline is a tentative description.

After puberty we begin to seek people outside the circle of our family, usually heterosexually but occasionally homosexually, to establish friendships with. We have more than that one friend with whom we share interests: we go on outings, play computer games, drink together and socialise. Initially we base our friendships on physical attraction, similarity of background and social class, education and mutual interests. We like our friends but we don't love them, and sex does not fit in these emotions.

Gradually over time one of our friends may emerge as somebody who becomes important to us emotionally, with whom we share feelings, ideas and the way we see the world. Is this love? It can be mistaken for love but it is not. We need to go deeper, to analyse the maturity of the person concerned. Are they reliable and trustworthy? Do they keep their promises? Do they let us down? Do they meet our needs? Now we are getting nearer to love and its sexual expression. Note that in this approach, personal affinity comes first and sexual intercourse second. There is a myth in society that we can explore love through sexual intercourse, but sexual intercourse tells us very little about the personality of the other person. They can be gentle and kind when making love but that does not mean that the rest of their personality is the same.

Finally we reach a point where we feel that we want to spend the rest of our lives with this person. This is the nearest subjective indication that we are really in love. The objective indication is if we are ready, to the best of our ability, to make a commitment to faithfulness and exclusivity for life, and to care for any potential children. Critics might ask how on earth we can make such a commitment at this early age, when we know nothing about the future. This is true, but what we do know is how we feel, and what we are prepared to accept with our heart, mind and will and stick to to the best of our ability. Of course, things may not work out like this, but it gives a rough outline of our understanding of what love means. It is not just romance, although it includes the romantic, nor is it merely a desire to have sex. It involves the whole of ourselves and ultimately this is what vows are about. They are the fullest expression of intended commitment to a person we love.

Falling in love or being in love is not a guarantee. We fall in love and out of love more than once, but the nearer we experience the fullness of the criteria I have just outlined, the nearer we are to our final destination of loving and therefore of intercourse.

Nowadays, the overwhelming majority of young people anticipate marriage by living together or cohabiting. Neither society nor Christianity know fully how to handle cohabitation, because until thirty years ago nearly everyone who was in love proceeded straight to marriage. But young people who have experienced their parents' broken marriages are cautious and want to test their compatibility. This will include sexual intercourse outside marriage, which does not fit with traditional Christian morality.

Recently, some theologians who have investigated cohabitation have compared it to the betrothal, a ceremony that committed a couple to each other and, prior to marriage, allowed intercourse and even childbearing, anticipating full marriage in Church. For at least a thousand years, in Christianity the essence of marriage was the commitment of a man to a woman with the intention of marriage but without a formal Church ceremony. The essential feature of the permanency we call marriage is and was a mutual, exclusive, faithful commitment. Thus, according to these theologians, preconjugal intercourse is moral. What is not moral is casual sex and non-preconjugal sex.

In this chapter, I have given an outline of how we might proceed from traditional sexual morality towards a morality in which the key is love. No doubt it needs to be further refined, but it is a step forward from the current situation in which, on the one hand, traditionalists insist on total abstinence before marriage, which very few observe, while on the other, the 'social wisdom' of the age says that anything goes providing that contraception is used.

CHAPTER SIX

HOMOSEXUALITY

A MINORITY OF MEN and women discover in early adolescence or soon after that they are attracted sexually and emotionally to their own sex. Same-sex relationships have been perceived and in some cases continue to be perceived as threatening both to society and to Christianity. Although attitudes are changing rapidly, some people still feel awkward and even hostile towards homosexuals, failing to understand and be able to handle their homosexual orientation. In these circumstances homosexuals can become a persecuted minority. In Britain, homosexuality was legalised in the 1960s and since 2000 homosexuals over 16 can live together and have sex. This is an advance, but fear and stigmatisation of homosexuality continue.

All the mainstream Christian denominations have problems with the issue of homosexuality because they are divided in their understanding of the meaning of the Bible's references to homosexual behaviour. In the past, an objection to homosexuality has been that the purpose of sex is the procreation of children, although this objection is now largely obsolete as we are discovering that sexual intercourse has other meanings and is primarily linked with love.

There is much debate over the subject and it now even threatens to split the Anglican communion, such is the strength of feelings it arouses. The Scriptures have been examined and re-examined and there is no consensus on their interpretation. Some theologians believe it is clear from a reading of the texts that homosexual acts are sinful, while other scholars interpret the texts differently. My view is that unless a particular biblical reference is embedded in love it does not truly express the word of God.

Given this background, I can proceed with the certainty that homosexuals, like everybody else, are children of God and need to receive and express love. This is their right as human beings, beloved by God. There can be no doubt that forging a loving relationship is the best social, psychological and emotional pattern for them.

As with a heterosexual couple, the partnership

needs to be enduring, faithful, exclusive and as far as possible permanent – not to imitate marriage, but because these are the conditions that allow love to flourish!

I have no doubt that such permanent relationships of love are good from a human point of view, because they encourage sustaining, healing and growth. What is clear, however, is that they are not marriages. They are a unique human relationship and in due course we will find a suitable and distinguishing term for them. Given that these men and women are children of God, destined for love with each other in this world and a continuation of love in the next, I have not an iota of doubt that such a loving relationship respects their human rights and the destiny of God for them.

Although there is considerable discussion and dissent on the matter, the mainstream Churches tend to teach that it is wrong for homosexuals to express their love sexually. Homosexuals who are practising Christians must use their own conscience, the supreme spiritual judgement of every human being, as regards how they express their love for each other.

CHAPTER SEVEN

FRIENDSHIP

THERE IS AN OVERLAP between marriage and friendship, best described by spouses feeling that their partner is also their best friend. This shows an intuitive awareness that, besides the roles partners play for each other as husband and wife, there is a distinctive relationship of friendship. But while everyone needs friendship, it comes into its own for single people.

Jesus called his apostles his friends (John 15:12–15) and Aelred of Rievaulx in the early middle ages believed that friendship was divine. The early middle ages offered a richness of Christian commentary on friendship, since when there has been relative silence!

All authentic friendships have something in common, namely companionship and togetherness. Togetherness, communication, demonstration of affection, affirmation and resolution of conflict may be central features of marital love, but they are also the building blocks of friendship.

Togetherness or companionship is of fundamental importance because it helps us to overcome loneliness and it gives us an opportunity to communicate. Communication affirms the friendship but it is far more important for other reasons. The first and most important of these is that it encourages trust, the key to all intimate relationships. Trust in turn establishes a basis for self-disclosure, which allows us to reveal a great deal about ourselves. Friends are the ones most likely to hear the phrase 'You are the first person I have ever told this!' This kind of disclosure can be comforting and reassuring, addressing our anxieties and allaying our guilt.

Friendship can help us to discover who we are, and to reflect on our identity by revealing and affirming it. Self-disclosure can help us to acquire a sense of our continuous and enduring identity. Friends may help us to know that we are the same yesterday, today and hopefully tomorrow. They do this by recognising, affirming and reaffirming who we are, and helping to remove uncertainties about ourselves. They can spot the gradual and evolving elements of who we are. Meeting again after a while (when we are ill, even after a day), they might say, 'You've changed', and we will want them to tell us what is different about us.

We need to be careful about self-disclosure because, if the friendship turns sour, our friend's knowledge can be used against us. Indeed real self-disclosure can only be confined to the few people we really trust.

True friends can do something fantastic – they can reach our unconscious when they say something about us which we did not know and are surprised to discover. Of course in the end we have to trust our own judgement because even the best of friends can be mistaken!

Friendship can also be a source of healing. Two of the most common psychological complaints are anxiety and depression, and a good friend who can reassure us and lift our mood is a tonic for our health.

Lastly, friendship is the basis for social help. Again and again we can turn to a friend and say 'Thank God you were there.' Millions of telephone calls and text messages give this reassurance every day, and what would any one of us do without the help of a friendly neighbour in emergencies?

At the heart of a good friendship, as with a good marriage, are the characteristics of continuity, reliability and predictability, which ensure that we can experience love, sometimes for a whole lifetime.

CHAPTER EIGHT

THE SEXUAL REVOLUTION

THE 1960s SAW a sexual revolution in Europe and North America. Almost every country in the developing world has now introduced legislation to legalise abortion, to make abortion and divorce easier and to outlaw sexual discrimination. These changes in the law reflected large-scale social changes blowing away many sexual taboos, liberalising sexual standards in the arts and encouraging far more provocative dress. All of this, coupled with the arrival of widespread contraception, opened the floodgates of sexual permissiveness. Liberals were and are delighted with a new era of sexual morality being ushered in, whilst conservatives were and are horrified.

What are the consequences of this revolution? On the positive side, centuries of fear, guilt and taboos associated with sex were set aside. Sexual pleasure was welcomed and, in Christian terms, one of God's most precious gifts was widely recognised and accepted. In all Christian denominations sex began to be seen in a different more positive light, linked with love.

On the negative side, sex was trivialised. Society has moved from looking at sexual activity with awe to treating it as another pleasure, similar to food and drink. Extensive research on sexuality in the twentieth century, such as that of Kinsey and Masters and Johnson, focused on the mechanical, biological aspects of sexual intercourse, and was preoccupied with facts, such as how often it occurred, in what positions and how maximum pleasure was achieved. Education at school emphasised the biological aspects and, where possible, the techniques of contraception.

The personal meaning of sexual intercourse and the emphasis on its loving and sacred aspects were almost totally ignored. And that's where we are at the present moment. Christianity, which for two thousand years had tragically undervalued this gift of God, retreated into the negativity of prohibitions, leading young people in particular to dismiss the Church as outmoded and irrelevant.

But young people, indeed most people, know

intuitively that sex and love are intimately connected. Christianity, which claims to be the sacred guardian of love, has failed to make the link. It has proclaimed love, but has not shown how ordinary men and women can live it in intimacy, every day. This is something which I have tentatively tried to do in this small book.

Instead, two main secular notions of love have emerged. The first is called 'liquid love', from the name of a book with that title by Zygmunt Bauman. The author attempts to portray love as fluid, transient and impermanent, focusing on the moment, and on realising the maximum of pleasure from casual meetings. The second has been formulated by Anthony Giddens, a leading sociologist, who has coined the phrase 'pure relationship', by which he means a situation where a social relationship is entered into for what can be derived by each partner from a sustained association with one another, and which is continued with only as long as it is thought by both parties to deliver enough satisfaction for each individual to stay in it.

These transient, disposable relationships are by no means the comprehensive ideologies of the age, but they do give a clue to the widespread presence of the sexual wilderness and of marital breakdown. Such transient relationships of love contradict all that modern psychology has demonstrated in the need for stability, continuity, reliability and mutual trust as the basis for love, security, healing and growth.

Such transitional relationships go against all the Christian norms of permanency in marriage and friendship and evoke a picture of unconscious, definite exploitation of human beings.

Unfortunately, in the last forty-five years the Roman Catholic Church has been preoccupied with contraception and the Anglican Church with women ministers, re-marriage in church and lately homo-sexuality. I am not saying that these issues are not important. What I am saying is that love is central to being human and to being a Christian and Christianity will not return to the centre of life in society until it stops focusing on important but peripheral issues and returns to the central issue of love in all human intimate relationships in the light of the sexual revolution of the twentieth century.